THE CASE FOR
CREATION

THE CASE FOR CREATION

by

WAYNE FRAIR

and

P. WILLIAM DAVIS

MOODY PRESS • CHICAGO

Library of Congress Catalog Card Number: 67-14381

ISBN: 0-8024-1185-1

Printed in the United States of America

CONTENTS

ACKNOWLEDGMENTS

We gratefully acknowledge the assistance of **Mrs.** Laurel Minch and Mrs. Karen Davis in the preparation of the manuscript. Thanks is also due **Mr. Robert Co-** canougher for the illustrations.

Preface

IN THE PAST DECADE numerous books on evolution have been written, including some works treating evolutionary theory from a more or less Christian point of view. Since the reader might well question the need for yet another addition to the already voluminous literature of scientific apologetics, the authors feel that a word of explanation is in order.

First it is an illusion to suppose that the problems which evolutionary doctrine raises for the Christian are well under control. This could be a very dangerous misconception. The Christian who is at ease regarding evolution is one who has no understanding of the true scope of the evangelical dilemma in this field of study. There has been no lack of speculation by Christians about the problems of origins, but most of these have not been based upon experimental attacks upon the problem, and hence have not grappled with the real issues raised by the evolutionists. For over a hundred years it has been the fashion to criticize while ignoring evidence and data which seem to support the evolutionary theory. However, a positive alternative has not been proposed which is biblically sound, intellectually satisfying, and *open to experimental demonstration*. All too often authors have blithely transfixed straw men with the omnipotent pen while the enemy has stalked them unawares. The doctrine of evolution in its present form is the creation of men of genius. To underestimate it and its impact is dangerous.

It is conceivable that we too may be accused of attempting to demolish a nonexistent foe, but our message is designed to produce a positive ring as well as, of necessity, to sound a negative undertone. We are presenting a position which, while bearing resemblance to some ancient opinions, still in our twentieth century is a very different approach to the problems of origins. At the time of this writing there are at best only a minuscule number of scientific programs aimed in our suggested direction. It is our aim to demonstrate this need and to enter a plea for research by Christians concerning the origins of life on earth. If this book stimulates either the initiation of well-conceived research programs or their financial support, it will have amply repaid the effort expended by the authors.

Second, scientific apologetics of the past have suffered no less at the hands of latitudinarians and concordists than at the hands of obscurantists. We are not sympathetic with the approach which attempts haphazardly to apply Scripture to the latest fashions of intellect or science. It is our firm conviction that the Scripture must be allowed to speak to man and that man must not presume to dictate to Scripture. We are not attempting to interpret (or misinterpret) the Bible so that it speaks the language of the twentieth century geologist or zoologist. This approach might impress naïve Christians, but it would not be accepted outside the church. In the long run it also would defeat its own purpose, by leaving the enemy in uncontested possession of the battlefield. Such an attempt really constitutes a search for the most graceful means of surrender.

We do not claim to have avoided either Scylla or Charybdis. Some passages doubtless will impress the reader as being obscurantist, and others will seem concordistic. It is our prayer, however, that our main ideas have been formulated after an honest examination of scientific data and proper biblical exegesis.

Finally, we have designed this book principally for the intelligent layman and for the student in the early years of his scientific training. Accordingly, we decided from the beginning to use a minimum of footnotes. This has limited the scholarly scope of our treatment but has, we hope, greatly increased its readability. Those who would delve more deeply into the subject should consult standard works. Some helpful books are listed in the selected Bibliography. Certain topics are not included in the scope of this paper (e.g., strictly geological matters such as dating and the Genesis flood). The authors are biologists and felt that these specialized topics should be treated by experts in these various fields.

1

Evolution and Science

EVERY AGE HAS POSSESSED certain unquestioned presuppositions which usually served as bases for the most popular philosophies of the day. Such a presupposition in our day is the theory of evolution. This concept has become the foundation of much scientific and political theory, formal philosophy, and even theology. Unquestioningly accepted in most quarters of society, evolutionary thought appears to be a cornerstone of civilization.

If this is the case, surely we ought to examine that cornerstone with care. If it is defective, the consequences one day could be disastrous. Disturbing evidence is accumulating to the effect that it has been unwise for us to allow this doctrine to become foundational; for it may be partially or wholly untrue.

In many high schools and colleges today evolution is treated as a fact. The evolutionary theory is indeed the product of men of genius and is the result of over a century of the most intense and serious intellectual effort. To the beginning student it seems to be an impregnable structure, for he is without the knowledge and experience to criticize it. It is the purpose of this book to show that evolutionary doctrine does not constitute an established fact and to present an alternative position

11

designed to challenge concerned individuals to discover more adequate explanations for the origins of living things.

The prevalent feeling in Western culture in recent centuries has been that growth and progress were inevitable. This optimistic mood promoted the belief that things in general were progressing positively and almost inevitably. Today we see all kinds of human activities and organizations starting from small and humble origins and increasing in complexity. So we have the feeling, perhaps unconsciously, that there is development and evolution in our world; for one meaning of the word evolution is "systematic development from the simple to the complex." "Biological evolution" usually refers to a progression in organisms from the simple to the relatively complex. Living organisms and extinct fossil forms are thought to be descendants of a relatively simple self-reproducing chemical or protoplasmic substance.

DARWINISM

When Charles Darwin over a century ago published his book *The Origin of Species,* people were in the mood to receive it. However, Darwin's theory of the evolution of life was not original. There are records of the beginnings of evolutionary thought in writings of Greeks such as Thales, Anaximander, Empedocles, and Aristotle hundreds of years before Christ. Nevertheless, it was not until the revival of classical and scientific learning in the seventeenth and eighteenth centuries that new evolutionary ideas were added to the ancient conceptions. This paved the way for the acceptance of Darwinism supported as it was by a vast array of original observations.

The Origin of Species went through five revisions at Darwin's hand. Darwin presented in it and in other writings his conclusions regarding the development of living things. In reading Darwin one receives a distinct impression that he was endeavoring to keep abreast of the latest discoveries and generally to face scientific issues fairly. His writings contain good scientific data which is acceptable today. However, some of his writings have been shown to be incorrect or at least open to considerable question in the light of modern knowledge. His works lack information on cytology (study of cells), physiology (study of function), and of course the newer sciences of biochemistry, biophysics, and biomathematics. For this reason they could not be expected to have endured in all their features as valid to this day.

Some of Darwin's embryological beliefs are now known to be untrue. Many of his anthropological ideas such as those regarding the development of religion and language have been shown to be incorrect. His ideas on the relationship between intelligence and sex are rejected today by competent psychologists (although some males still cling to them tenaciously), for he stated that ". . . the average of mental power in man must be above that of woman," and that through sexual selection ". . . man has ultimately become superior to woman."[1]

[1] C. Darwin, *The Descent of Man.* Vol. II: *The Origin of Species* and *The Descent of Man* (New York: Random House, Inc.), pp 873-74.

These ideas were related to his erroneous concepts regarding heredity, for he invented bodies known as *gemmules* in order to account, as he thought, for observed hereditary data. We will return to this subject later. Understandably, modern concepts of heredity involving genetic ratios, chromosome studies, deoxyribonucleic acid (DNA) and many other new concepts are very different from anything Darwin could have proposed. It is undeniable, however, that the major features of Darwin's evolutionary thought have endured to this day. Darwin's evolutionary ideas were accepted by many scientists of his day, but a considerable number of great scientists including Owen, von Baer, Wigand, Mivart, Agassiz, and Sedgwick rejected his theories. Today no informed scientist believes exactly as Darwin did, but the most popular current evolutionary views are Darwinian, although modified in the light of present knowledge.

In recent years there has been a growing tendency in many areas (for example, taxonomy) to use other than evolutionary approaches to scientific data. This has happened because of the misapplication of Darwinism as it spread, and because many exceptions to evolutionary generalizations have been found. Although the doctrine of evolution was presented to account for changes among living things, its implications have been extended in many directions. Unfortunately, it has been utilized by those who wish to discredit the Bible and destroy man's faith in God. Wherever this has been successful there has been a decline in morals and in spiritual vitality.

Darwin's teachings also have been extended to justify taking unfair advantage of others. This is known as social Darwinism, and was expounded by Herbert Spencer even before Darwin published his evolutionary ideas. Spencer imagined an evolutionary social struggle at all levels in which the greatest advancement was secured by ruthless and unethical competition. In this way, by analogy with animal competition and "survival of the fittest," many unscrupulous activities could be justified. Teachings of such leaders as Nietzsche and Hitler have contained ideas consistent with social Darwinism. Fortunately this social application of evolution is not now popular among peoples of the free world.

Another popular belief growing out of Darwin's writings in the past century held "wild" tribes to be composed of people who were intermediate between apes and civilized man. Many people thought that culture (including religion) had evolved through a series of patterns, all of which were to be seen among living peoples. According to this teaching, lineal evolution began with the savages. Contrary to these ideas, recent studies in cultural anthropology have indicated that regardless of the degree of civilization, members of the human race possess a basic physiological, psychological, and spiritual unity.

The popular nineteenth century view held so-called "primitive" or stone age men to be intermediate between apes and modern Europeans with regard to language, arts, and intelligence. It is now recognized that their languages are often more intricate and expressive than our own.[2] Great skill is evidenced in much of their drawing, carving, weaving, and pottery. Their music is often of complex and subtle rhythmic structure, though we may not appreciate it because our ears are attuned to our own concepts of melody and harmony. The culture of stone age men living some 7,000 years ago is as sophisticated as that of many advanced "primitive" tribes today. In these, as in all cultures of living men, there is belief in the supernatural and in life after death.

When adequate testing procedures are utilized, the intelligence of modern primitive peoples approximates our own. This intelligence and the presence of human culture practically and readily distinguish man from all animals. During the twentieth century many of the erroneous ideas spawned from early evolutionary presuppositions in anthropology have been corrected. So the chief scientific quest in anthropology today is not the determination of which race of men is most like the apes, but rather the study of the diversified patterns of culture and physique as presently found among men. The most fruitful scientific endeavors in anthropology have been those conducted *within* the family of man himself.

Similarly, biological studies of animals are most fruitful when conducted within the species of the

[2] "The fact is that many 'primitive' languages aren't any more primitive than most of the rest of the culture; indeed, they are often a great deal more complex and more efficient than the languages of the so-called higher civilizations." Ashley Montagu, *Man: His First Million Years* (rev. ed.; New York: New American Library, 1962), p. 102.

animal in question. Scientific efforts which involve a study of variations within specific groups of animals are, for the most part, scientifically valid. They may be verified much more readily from an objective point of view than those studies which have attempted to relate large groups of organisms to each other. General similarities which exist among large groups of animals or members of differing groups such as dogs and rabbits, or cats and mice, for instance, can be explained as originating in a basic design impressed upon and inherent within all living creatures.

NATURE OF SCIENCE

We have seen that as the doctrine of Darwinian evolution spread, its implications touched many areas of thought. There are many reasons for its misapplication and its present position of prominence in the scientific world. One of the important reasons is that the methods and techniques of science are not well understood. Often a statement that something is "scientific" is taken by the layman to mean it is *certain,* but this shows an incorrect comprehension of the true situation.

Science itself differs from the products of science. Most of the technological differences between our way of life and those of past civilizations are due to improved methods of exploiting the environment with which science has provided us. The products of science are, from a practical point of view, *tools.* The use of most of these tools—such as bulldozers or airplanes—is obvious. The use of others is less apparent. For example, a theory can be considered a useful tool—a key to nature which opens up new roads to knowledge. However, because it *is* a tool, any theory has certain limitations. It must be used intelligently, it should be improved as knowledge accumulates, and it should fall into disuse when a more effective tool is invented. Let us consider the origin of theories and their use, for a more basic tool of science hardly exists.

A theory is conceived and born after the accumulation of data, not all of which is necessarily discovered by one man. It is unlikely that any major theory could be formulated without the help of many past investigators. When sufficient information on a topic accumulates, the scientific investigator attempts to make a *generalization*. A generalization is a statement encompassing all observed data in summary form. The earliest form of a generalization is termed a *hypothesis*. When observations confirming a hypothesis accumulate, the hypothesis becomes a *theory;* and a theory unchallenged and consistently supported by facts is called a *law* after a considerable lapse of time.

As more data accumulates a generalization may pass from hypothesis to theory and then to law. But in this process the generalization does not become fact; the likelihood of its being correct merely increases, or as it is commonly stated, it has higher statistical probability. If any observation (even though seemingly trivial) ever conflicts with the generalization, or hypothesis, the scientist is left with two major alternatives: (1) Discard the hypothesis and search for another, or (2) Attempt to find some plausible explanation for the observation in accord with the hypothesis.

There is no major scientific hypothesis or theory of any age that has escaped either or both of these fates. An interesting and humorous example concerns one investigator who persuaded a slime mold organism to crawl through a pinhole and hang threadlike from it. This thread of protoplasm twisted in a clockwise direction nineteen times. The experimenter felt that he was on the track of a fundamental biological law. Unfortunately, on the twentieth trial, the slime mold twisted in a counter-clockwise direction.

The history of science is filled with discarded and amended theories. Those which have been amended so often as to lose their original identity become like the proverbial pair of pants that ended up more patch than pants. Sometimes theories are abandoned entirely—when an involved patching process raises serious doubt as to the validity of the basic concept involved. Often a theory seems so well grounded that it is unchallenged for generations, only to be upset by the uncovering of new data inconsistent with the old. Neither hypothesis, theory, nor law is in the same realm as absolute truth. All three rest upon a perennially shaky foundation, and all are vulnerable to uncomfortable facts.

As Christians we believe that only God can know the universe as it *really is*. We are limited by our senses and our minds, and know the universe only as it *appears* to us. In science we do not believe in generalizations because we know them to be *true;* we believe in them only because they are *credible* to us. Several competing explanations for the same phenomenon may be equally attractive, and often none of them can be proven false. Who can say which, if any, of them reflects reality? Usually we apply the principle of logic called "Occam's razor" and accept the simplest explanation, but for all we *know*, this may not be the best answer. And even when no alternative explanation exists, does that mean that no alternative is possible? Thus we are forever uncertain in our understanding of the universe; our most assured conclusions are nevertheless tentative if we depend only upon our own rational faculties.

The purpose of this excursus has been to show that no scientific statement is unassailable, and no theory should be regarded as final. Now the theory of evolution, like other theories, depends upon the interpretation of observations. Only in a limited sense is it subject to any kind of experimental test or confirmation, because of its basic nature. Evolution, as commonly understood, is currently undergoing modification; and we believe that this will lead to the eventual rejection of it in its present form.

Evolutionists often differentiate between what they consider the "fact" of evolution and the "theories" of evolution. The fact supposedly consists of observed changes in animal and plant fossils over a period of time (geological evidence), whereas theories of evolution attempt to explain how the changes have occurred. The theories deal with mechanisms of evolution such as natural selection and genetics. Bearing this distinction in mind, we shall see that reliable conclusions are difficult to draw from the fossil record, which contains many gaps. There seems to be little justification for the popular practice of presenting unrestricted evolution as fact or law. The so-called "fact" of evolution cannot be shown to be factual, and therefore should not be presented as such.

2

Reasons for Similarities

SIMILARITY AND ANCESTRY

MACROEVOLUTION is the form of evolution usually taught in high schools, secular colleges, and universities today.[1] It is what the British scholar Kerkut calls "the general theory of evolution." It asserts that nonliving substance gave rise to the first living material which subsequently reproduced and diversified to produce all the *major* categories of extinct and extant organisms. Most of the remainder of this booklet is devoted to a brief discussion and critical evaluation of this teaching. The arguments for macroevolution generally fall into two somewhat overlapping categories: historical and comparative. In the historical arguments attempts are made to show from the fossil record that major groups of animals had ancestors in common or were related in some way. Comparative arguments are concerned with similarities of anatomy, physiology, development, biochemistry, and behavior. Comparative arguments depend upon the *assumption* that similarities among animals or plants indicate common ancestry.

---

[1] The term megaevolution is used by some to designate evolution of the largest categories of organisms, and the term macroevolution to refer to somewhat smaller categories. We, however, prefer to use the term macroevolution in its earlier sense to refer to all of the so-called large changes and to distinguish it only from microevolution, which refers to small

We must emphasize that this fundamental assumption is *not* an established fact, and indeed, even evolutionists use it only with great restrictions. For example, more similarities exist among a raccoon, fox, dog, and wolf than between any of these and a cat. However, the fact that animals can be sorted into categories does not necessarily indicate that the animals were of common descent. A hyena appears to be quite doglike, but on the basis of its teeth, it generally is considered to be related to the civets, a group closely akin to the cats. The principle that similarity indicates common ancestry is inadequate in many ways. Often organisms with striking similarities are clearly unrelated. Such facts present no problem for the creationist, but the evolutionist must explain them in terms of his theory. The concepts of *convergence* and *mimicry* have been the major explanations attempted.

Convergence refers to the resemblance of two animals of separate ancestry which have adapted to comparable habitats so as to resemble one another closely. For example, evolutionists do not regard the pouched animals of Australia as closely related to the mammals of the rest of the world, but as closely parallel to them in form and habits. Included among those Australian animals believed to show convergence are marsupial "mice," "wolves," and "moles." The nature of the complication or contradiction introduced by the existence of such

changes. In this booklet instead of using the term microevolution, we use *diversification*, which denotes small changes, namely those which produced the multiformity of living things from the uniformity of the original creation.

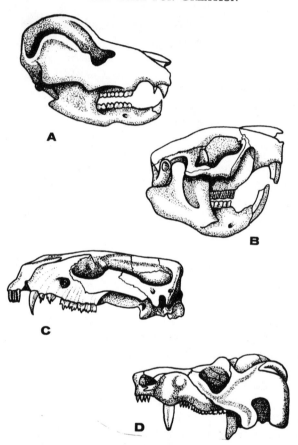

Figure 1—Similar Adaptations in mammal-like reptiles and mammals. A—*Bienotherium,* after Romer. B—Beaver, original. C—*Dasyurus,* after Parker and Haswell. D—*Diademodon,* original.

Although A bears considerable resemblance to B, and C to D, nevertheless these forms are not considered by evolutionists to be at all closely related.

creatures is this: How can an evolutionist be certain that supposedly common characteristics which he takes to be evidence of common ancestry are not in fact examples of convergence? This is an internal difficulty in the theory of evolution.

The mammal-like reptiles serve well as another case in point. Frequently these extinct creatures resemble mammals in astonishing detail, yet the majority of them are not considered by paleontologists to be ancestral to mammals for one reason or another. From Figure 1 it is possible to distinguish clearly the fossil rodentlike *Bienotherium* from the modern beaver even though they share many of the same structural features such as the massive coronoid process of the jaw, grinding molar teeth, heavy cutting incisors, and even a small hump in the posterior ventral border of the eye socket. The fossil *Diademodon* also shares many characteristics with the modern Australian marsupial *Dasyurus*. Points of resemblance are the sharp tearing incisors, the space (diastema) between those incisors and the heavy stabbing canine teeth, the posterior grinding molars, and a general shape characteristic of carnivores.

Similarities among these animals are believed to have resulted from convergence rather than genetic relationship only because the overall differences (or certain differences arbitrarily regarded as being of paramount importance) are as marked or more marked than the similarities. From these differences it is concluded that they are not closely related, but if the differences were minor, anatomists would suppose that they shared a proximate common ancestry. Future studies may demonstrate that many animals now thought to be closely related share common characteristics not because of relationship but rather because of what is popularly called convergence. Examples of this type add weight to the concept that animals were separate and genetically *un*related at their inception.

Mimicry is similar to convergence in that it involves the close superficial resemblance of animals unrelated to one another. For instance, certain types of flies are marked in such a way that they superficially resemble bees. Evolutionists believe that such markings and color patterns are protective because predators would be less likely to molest those possessing them. Thus two animals that are unrelated or at best distantly related could show resemblance because of mimicry.

Even though evolutionists themselves from time to time have pointed out the questionable nature of the assumption of close relationship based upon similarity, there has been a general tendency toward this type of deduction. So now virtually all comparative studies of physiology, biochemistry, embryology, and behavior proceed on the same questionable assumption as that concerning the adult anatomical structure; i.e., that a present similarity indicates common ancestry.

We prefer an interpretation of data which resembles the classical approach previously used by experts. Our approach is progressive and from the scientific standpoint more closely reaches an objective position which is subject to verification (or disproof). Essentially, this position is that rather than a continuum of related forms there were certain basic phylogenetically unrelated organisms which gave rise to the vast array of extinct and extant living things. (See Figure 2.) Similarities exist because of a *common creative plan* or design according to which basic organisms were created.

REPRODUCTION AND SURVIVAL

A fair statement of Darwinian evolution could be: "The systematic elimination of some randomly occurring but inheritable variants by environmental forces, and the promotion of other variants by environmental factors resulting in semipermanent novelties." Darwin felt that some organisms would be eliminated from life by the multitude of hazards existing in changing habitats. Other organisms better fitted by heredity and experience for survival would do well. These latter would produce relatively more descendants, and their types eventually would predominate in the population. Notice that the crucial concept is not just that of the survival of the "fittest" individuals but their *superior reproduction*. The fittest might not always appear such to us. The only judge of superiority would be the blind hand of the natural environment which would give such individuals a selective advantage. This doctrine was called natural selection; it includes not only survival of the fittest but also (in particular) their superior reproduction.

Imagine a board in which a variety of holes are punched of different sizes and shapes. If we pile assorted shaped blocks on this board, only those

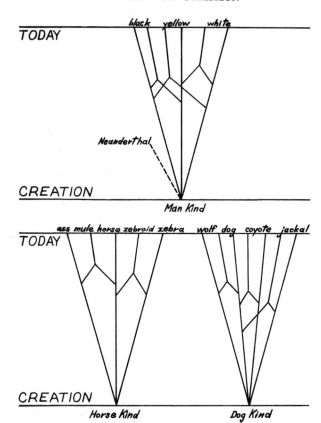

Figure 2—diversification of modern varieties from their ancestral created "kinds" (modified after Marsh). In this book we have not treated the biblical flood, but presumably it would have destroyed most of the types which had diversified from the time of creation until the flood so that subsequent to this deluge only certain of the various types belonging to each grouping would have produced further diversification.

which fit the niches in the board will remain on it when it is tilted. Again, we might compare natural selection to a sieve. Only particles of a certain size will be retained by the sieve; others will fall through. The environment exercises a selective effect upon the population of organisms. Those best adapted to it will fare best in the competition of life. Ultimately they will predominate, and the entire number of such organisms will be adapted to the habitat they occupy.

Darwin was unable to explain the origin of variations. He devised a generalization to account for their origin which resembled, oddly enough, certain aspects of the theory of Lamarck involving inheritance of acquired characteristics. Darwin devised the hypothesis of *pangenesis*. According to this hypothesis an organ affected or impinged upon by the environment would respond by giving off particles (gemmules). These particles were supposedly hereditary in the sense that they could determine the characteristics which the next generation would inherit. The environment would impinge upon an organ; the organ would give off gemmules which would move to the sex organs where they would affect the nature of sex cells.

It has been remarked that Darwin would have benefited immensely from a meeting with the Austrian monk Gregor Mendel. This brilliant scientist was the original discoverer of the principles of heredity that bear his name. The details of his experiments are well known and need not be repeated here. Suffice it to say that he established the particulate theory of genetics in which hereditary units in reproductive cells of the organism determine characteristics of the offspring. Results of his research helped overthrow the "blending" theory of inheritance in which it was assumed that offspring had characteristics intermediate between those possessed by their parents. Mendel did not, however, ascertain the mechanism by which inheritance particles (commonly called genes[2]) could be altered. This was not discovered until recent times.

Now it is believed that genes (and chromosomes) can suddenly change, or *mutate*, and give their possessors characteristics not found in their parents or other ancestors. Generally such mutations are disadvantageous to the organism, and it is easy to see why. An organism is so delicately adjusted to its environment that any change is likely to affect it negatively. Imagine making a random change in the design of a watch. Anyone who has tried to repair one for himself will probably appreciate that such a change is not likely to be for the better. Nevertheless, a beneficial change is possible in rare instances. Similarly, in living organisms favorable mutations are rare, but some observed mutations seem to be favorable under certain conditions.·

It is important to realize, however, that a mutation which seems to be favorable is useful only in a narrow range of environments. A dark colored moth is better off than a light colored one only against a dark colored background where it is in-

---

[2] In modern genetic parlance the term *cistron* can refer operationally to what is commonly thought of as a gene. Chemically we are dealing with DNA.

conspicuous. Hence a mutation is only advantageous if it brings the organism into more nearly perfect adjustment with its surroundings. If an environment is changing, a new mutation will have a better chance of being favorable than it would under static conditions. An excellent example is the resistance which insect populations often develop to insecticides. The mutation is disadvantageous in a normal environment because of seemingly deleterious side effects. In an insecticide-saturated environment, however, the insecticide-resistant mutation is the only one that has any chance of survival at all. It can be shown mathematically that any advantageous mutation, however slight the advantage, will eventually spread throughout a population and dominate it.[3] Thus in a heavily sprayed area most mosquitoes inevitably become resistant to the insecticide employed. Conversely, if spraying is suspended for a few years, this mutation will decline in frequency in the population and the mosquitoes once again will become susceptible. Alternatively, another insecticide might be used to which the population may in time also develop a resistance. A mutation is only advantageous or makes the organism "more fit" in the evolutionary sense when it enables the organism to survive and reproduce more satisfactorily in its present environment.

Populations of insects, bacteria, and other organisms have been changed through mutations inside

---

[3] Certain phenomena like drift or meiotic drive, however, in special circumstances can oppose spread of a feature which confers selective advantage.

the laboratory and out, and these changes have been noted by competent observers. It is important to realize, however, that these are only relatively minor changes in organisms and illustrate the mechanism of diversification. Radical changes in organisms (the changes for which evolutionary theory must account) have never been observed to occur by mutations in the laboratory or anywhere else.

An organism is not a bundle of isolated characteristics. Any radical change in a single characteristic would have to be accompanied by a myriad of other changes occurring at the same time or the creature would be a monstrosity and unable to survive because of internal inconsistencies. It would be thrown completely out of adjustment with itself and with its surroundings by any major isolated change. The chances of a concert of appropriate mutations occurring together and staying together is infinitesimally small. Transitions from one major group of animals to another would have to be of such a nature. It is no surprise that they have not been observed. We venture to suggest that they have not occurred.

VESTIGES AND FOSSIL DISCONTINUITIES

Evolutionists have pointed out that certain structures often found in organisms seem to have no functions. These are called *vestigial organs*, and they may be distinguished from rudimentary structures such as nipples in male primates which normally do not develop. The presence of so-called vestigial organs is supposed to indicate that the animal possessing them is descended from an ancestor in which the organs were useful. Blind cave fish which have remnants of eyes, and flies with a hereditary stubby-shriveled wing condition appear to have true vestigial organs. These and similar degenerations apparently have resulted from mutations, and they may result in a distinct disadvantage unless the organisms are in a protective environment. When hereditary changes are small enough to permit survival and reproduction, vestiges may remain. However, these vestigal structures at best are indicative of changes within limits; they are usually degenerative changes within a species.

A better name for some of these so-called vestigial organs would be "organs of unknown function." The list of human structures thought to be vestigial has shrunk greatly in recent years. Formerly, for example, the thyroid gland, thymus, tonsils, and appendix were regarded as vestigial and of no use to the modern human being. Now all of these have been shown to be vital, or at least useful (if not diseased) to the person possessing them. The thyroid gland releases important hormones; the thymus appears to be important during early life for a normal development of the body's protective chemical substances (antibodies); and the tonsils and appendix further function in protecting the body against disease. Even the coccyx, the supposed remnant of a prehensile tail, serves as a point of anchorage for several muscles. It may not be vital, but it is definitely useful.

One of the arguments for evolution that has been

most difficult for Christians to answer is the historical argument. The fossil record is most impressive; no one who has visited a great museum can deny the reality of the rich and varied forms of life which have inhabited our planet in the past. But viewed as a whole, the fossil record reveals one of the strongest supports for creation.

Gaps are almost always present in the fossil record where a gradual transition from one major group of organisms to another would be expected according to macroevolutionary theory. Some of these gaps are more striking than others. For example, the ancestry of sharks is somewhat unclear to the evolutionists because of an absence of intermediate forms between them and their possible ancestors. Critical review of the published materials shows a similar gap between the allegedly most primitive land tetrapods and their supposed fish ancestors. Very striking among animals is the total lack of plausible ancestors for the extinct aquatic reptiles known as ichthyosaurs. An outstanding example in the botanical kingdom is the class of angiosperms (vascular plants with enclosed seeds). This class of plants makes up about 85 percent of all plant life in the world today. These plant forms seem to have made a sudden appearance, and there are no known forms with sufficient similarity to have been their direct ancestors. A similar situation exists for the class Insecta which contains about 80 percent of all species of animal life. Even though examples of gaps could be multiplied, we wish to point out that in some cases what may appear to the creationist as a vast gulf between groups of organisms may appear to the evolutionist as a trifling discontinuity.[4] The reality of these gaps is, however, well attested by the efforts of the evolutionists to account for them in theory. Both Goldschmidt's saltation and Simpson's quantum evolution are examples of efforts made by evolutionists to account for the existence in the fossil record of hiatuses which become more, not less, pronounced with continued study and collection of fossils.

We believe that gaps exist because a certain limited number of "kinds" of organisms were created, as recorded in the book of Genesis. These kinds were separated from other kinds by gaps and subsequently diversified to become the numerous organisms we now know either as fossils or as living forms.

---

[4] It should be recognized that what one man considers a "gap" another considers to be bridged by some "link." For example, *Archeopteryx*, a fossil toothed bird, is generally regarded as a link between birds and their ancestral reptiles. There is no reason why a form like *Archeopteryx* could not have been created specially; and there is no reason, from a purely logical point of view, why this is not as likely an explanation for its existence as the evolutionary one. Even some evolutionists do not regard *Archeopteryx* as ancestral to modern birds.

In most other cases it is not possible to present even as good a case for links as the above. Real and seemingly unbridgeable gaps have been found in the so-called "history" of almost all major groups of animals, vertebrates and invertebrates.

3

Comparative Arguments

CLASSIFICATION

BEFORE THE RISE of recent evolutionary theories which postulate the relationship of all living things to unknown common ancestors, scientists sought to determine natural groupings of plants and animals, without supposing that these groups were derived from common ancestors. It was with this approach that our present system of classification was originated by Linnaeus (who did not believe in evolution)[1] and underwent the bulk of its development. In recent years, however, some scientists have attempted to inject unproved evolutionary presuppositions into classification studies, thus producing what has been called evolutionary taxonomy. Taxonomy is a division of science dealing with classification. Many leading taxonomists are presently objecting to evolutionary taxonomy on the grounds that it is too subjective, and thus not scientifically valid. They rightly feel that the best practice is to classify organisms not according to their assumed ancestors, but rather according to their *present nature*, which involves phenotype (appearance) and genetic criteria.[2]

---

[1] Linnaeus did, however, recognize that there had been some changes (diversification) from the time the original kinds were created.

[2] See for example B. Glass (ed.), *Survey of Biological Prog-*

Some of the most recent classification procedures are being employed by numerical taxonomists who endeavor to establish classification on a numerical basis utilizing computers. For instance they make many measurements on body regions of organisms. These dimensions are then fed into a computer in a program designed to reveal relationships of the organisms. Because of the ways numerical taxonomists have set up their programs, evolutionists have sometimes accused them of being against evolution. Numerical taxonomists have averred their innocence and assured them that their particular non-evolutionary approaches are most fair. Unfortunately, some scientists seem to think taxonomic systems are sacred and use them as proof of evolutionary ideas. A brief survey of modern taxonomic procedures should suffice to dispel this idea.

In classification, the species is the most definitive major category in modern usage. Every animal or plant belongs to a species. All members of a species are similar in structure and function and usually they do not breed with members of other species to produce fertile offspring. Different but "related" species belong in turn to larger categories including genus, family, order, class, and phylum. For example, the house cat is classified as follows:

PHYLUM *Chordata*—all animals possessing at some time in their life cycle pharyngeal pouches, a notochord, and a dorsal tubular nerve cord.

ress, Vol. IV, R. E. Blackwelder, "Animal Taxonomy and the New Systematics" (New York: Academic Press, 1962), pp. 1-57. Also R. R. Sokal and P. H. A. Sneath, *Principles of Numerical Taxonomy* (San Francisco: W. H. Freeman, 1963).

SUBPHYLUM *Vertebrata*—all those animals which possess vertebrae.

CLASS *Mammalia*—all those animals which have internally regulated body temperature, possess hair, and suckle their young.

ORDER *Carnivora*—all those mammals whose teeth are adapted to a predatory mode of life but which are not insectivores.

FAMILY *Felidae*—all those carnivora with retractile claws, lengthy tail, and a certain tooth arrangement.

GENUS *Felis*—the true cats

SPECIES *domestica*.

The basic system of classification in use today is little more than two hundred years old, and men are continually adding new names and changing organisms from one category to another. Some taxonomists are called lumpers because they prefer to classify organisms into larger categories whereas the splitters prefer to multiply the number of smaller groupings.

The evolutionary argument from taxonomy, when reduced to its elements, states in effect that (1) it is possible to arrange organisms in groups according to their similarities and that (2) these similarities indicate common ancestry. Since taxonomy is basically a method of grouping organisms according to certain of their similarities, we expect taxonomic categories to be fundamentally homogeneous and to differ more or less from other taxonomic groupings. Of course it is true that many organisms, especially in very similar groupings, may indeed share a common ancestry, but this cannot be shown on the basis of taxonomy itself. Rather than indicating an evolutionary relationship, the taxonomic system merely constitutes a proof that the human mind has the ability to categorize.

The system is man-made; but it is very useful. It exists because men can easily recognize that groups of organisms are separated by natural gaps from other groups. Thus the overall pattern of nature bears testimony that distinct categories do in fact exist. Each distinct grouping had a starting point in time and certain members have been modified by a limited number of small changes since that time. One of the tasks of the Christian biologist is to determine the natural categories. We believe that God created certain kinds of animals and plants. Exactly what these were and how much they have changed since then are matters that remain to be discovered.

EMBRYOLOGY

Another widely discussed variation of the comparative argument is the embryological approach. Like other comparative arguments, it depends upon the assumption that common characteristics imply common ancestry. However, in embryology we observe that these common characteristics are not static, but change during the development of the organism from a fertilized egg until birth (or hatching).

In 1828 Karl Ernst von Baer published hypotheses regarding embryonic resemblance. He observed the similarity of the embryos of mammals, birds, lizards, and snakes during their earlier stages. The younger the embryos were, the more alike they appeared to be. This belief in the similarity of young embryos was based upon carefully observed facts. Then a *false* doctrine arose that was based upon some of the same facts.

For many years this doctrine led many earnest biologists down a false trail from which, even to this day, some have not returned. The idea took such a hold on embryology that it was considered a law, which is a term properly used only for thoroughly established concepts. When the term "biogenetic law" is used today, it usually refers to this doctrine. A terse statement of the "law" is "ontogeny recapitulates phylogeny," that is, the embryonic history of the individual outlines the actual developmental history of the race. Emphasized by Darwin in 1859, the doctrine was vigorously spread by Ernst Haeckel, starting with a publication of his in 1866. Unfortunately some of his work involved scientific dishonesty, which is now recognized. But in spite of this, certain of his diagrams have been reproduced uncritically through generations of textbooks to further the teaching of evolution.

The "biogenetic law" teaches that as an embryo develops it passes through the stages experienced by the adult organism in its long process of evolution. If we lined up a series of early to late human embryos, for example, we could see a fish stage, amphibian stage, reptile stage, up to mammal stage. Thus, embryonic life would resemble an abbreviated "moving picture" of the entire history of the race. This doctrine is referred to as recapitulation because it pertains to a summing up of race history. Recapitulation studies appeared to be ideal for solving evolutionary problems, and both plant and animal materials were studied in the light of this principle. It was even used to study human social practices. As study progressed, however, the list of exceptions became greater than the amount of data confirming the idea.

The human embryo, for instance, passes through a stage resembling a fish. But it does not closely resemble a mature fish; the resemblance is only vague, for there is no fishlike tail and no fins. There are, however, pharyngeal (or so-called "gill") pouches in the same region where a fish will develop gills. In the human embryo (as well as in mammals, birds, and reptiles in general) these pouches are useful, for they will develop into important structures such as the ear chamber, tonsils, parathyroid glands, and thymus. The human embryo never really has gills; the cartilaginous bars separating the pouches contain blood vessels necessary for the passage of blood to the head and dorsal aorta. The pharyngeal pouches of the human embryo are similar only to those found in the *embryonic* fish.

Interestingly enough, the exact reverse of the Darwinian idea of recapitulation frequently occurs. Instead of finding in an embryo the adult stages of the supposed species ancestor, we see in the *adult* an embryonic stage of this supposed ancestor. For instance, man has a poorly developed coat of body hair compared to apes and does not have ridges over the eyes as apes have. In these traits he actually resembles a very *young* ape whose hair and brow ridges have not yet developed. This reverse of recapitulation has been found in many studies of such diverse organisms as molluscs, insects, and chordates.

Most modern biologists no longer hold the recapitulation view which was popular fifty years ago. Most recognize now that in general this doctrine is invalid and therefore unreliable. Instead of holding the view that embryonic organisms show stages of adult forms which supposedly preceded them in evolution, we find it much safer to return to the earlier and simpler views of von Baer, that many very early embryos are similar and that they become more and more dissimilar as they grow older.

During growth and development each structure has its own function. Structures appear on the embryonic stage for varying lengths of time. Some stay essentially as they are; others change or disappear, but each plays its part in the drama of embryonic life. Structures of the pharyngeal region of man produce parts of the ears, mouth, and neck. The notochord is absent in most adult vertebrates, but if it is removed from the embryo, no central nervous system will develop. The first kidney (pronephros), which later disappears, affects growth of other structures which do remain and function throughout life and which would not develop unless it were present. Structures in embryos are not present just because supposed evolutionary ancestors had them; they are not merely useless vestiges left over. In fact, scientists are cautious about saying that any structure found in any stage of the life cycle (even in the adult) is a vestige, because often (as already mentioned) valuable functions for such structures have been discovered. The simpler explanation is that structures are present because they have a part to play in the life of the organism, and in general the more similar the distinct organisms are, the more similar their embryological development is likely to be.

Comparative embryology can be of use in the classification of groups of animals. In certain cases when adult organisms have shown great differences, embryological similarities have given clues to their classification. For example, the adult of the barnacle, *Sacculina,* is unlike other organisms, but its embryology is like that of other barnacles. This case, however, is an exception, and in general similar adults have similar developmental patterns. These patterns along with adult characteristics are of aid in determining with what group the particular organism should be placed.

Living things begin development as single cells and increase in complexity as they get older. We would expect that embryos would be more like the adult form the older they become. Four men with pieces of wood or bars of soap can start to carve a fish, turtle, dog, and cat. The further they go according to their plans, the easier it is to tell what they are making. At first all the blocks look alike. Later they look less alike, and still later we can see that the one is a fish, or another a turtle. But in carvings of similar animals (such as dog and cat) one might not be able to tell which was which until they were almost finished.[3]

---

[3] This illustration has a basis in embryological theory and is not chosen in a cavalier manner. In mathematics *stochastic variables* are of such a nature that every event that occurs limits the possibilities of the succeeding event, which in turn limits the number of possible events that may succeed *it,* and so on. A driver in California heading east could go to any number of states, but once he has reached Kansas, for example, he can only go to the states which lie east of Kansas. In eastern Pennsylvania his immediate choices would be limited to New York and New Jersey. If he arrives in southern New Jersey he can reach no other state by continuing to drive in an easterly direction.

Similarly, an embryo begins as an undifferentiated mass of cells. In vertebrates a bit of tissue from a very young embryo can be made to develop into any adult structure characteristic of its species. Normally a bit of tissue might turn into an eye, but by surgically transplanting it to different locations in the body of the embryo it can be made to develop into heart, for instance, or kidney. Its *potencies* (potentialities) are virtually unlimited. As the embryo matures, however, the potencies of various tissues become more restricted. In time the eye region will be able to form nothing but eye. Eye nerves will then develop nowhere but in the eye itself and from eye tissue. If the heart region and eye region had been exchanged early enough, however, the eye nerve would have developed in the transplanted heart tissue, which would by then have become not heart but eye. Scientists have thus discovered that embryonic potencies become more limited as the embryo matures. This is an example of stochastic development.

Evolution is also supposed to be a stochastic process. A dog could never have evolved from a bat, for both are too specialized to have given rise to one another. Their potencies would have become limited by the passage of evolutionary time. However, an insectivore, a most generalized mammal, is thought by evolutionists to have given rise ultimately to both. Evolutionary theory supposes that the common ancestors of animals were the simple or generalized progenitors of more specialized forms. Because of the stochastic nature of embryonic development, the earlier stages of embryos are generalized, and for this reason tend to resemble one another. Coincidentally they also tend to resemble the supposed com-

Thus it is with embryos. They develop from simple to complex, from like to more unlike, according to the plans originally laid out by the Creator and now stamped in the genes within every cell. The various parts of the embryos do their own jobs at certain stages in development, and chemicals called organizers function in their own particular, wonderful ways. Each organism bears considerable resemblance to others of the same group in which God created it, but such similarities do not necessarily imply a common ancestry.

Some further clarification of the condition of early embryonic stages is necessary. In addition to the unobservable differences among the DNA patterns of the various genes, there are a number of observable morphological and physiological group distinctives which may be seen from the earliest embryological stages. It is true that each embryo starts as a single cell, but these cells are not all the same; there are differences, for example, in the quantity and distribution of yolk. There are also differences among the cleavage patterns of cells as they multiply in number.

Later in development we find differences in mesoderm and coelom formation. Mesodern is the middle of three major germ layers of the chordate embryo. From it such things as muscles, blood, and bones will develop. The body cavity, or coelom, always begins as a cavity within the mesoderm. Consider

---

mon ancestor of the forms being compared, simply because if such an ancestor existed it would be generalized. Therefore, the nature of the supposed proof offered by the recapitulation argument rests upon a fortuitous resemblance.

the formation of mesoderm in three chordates and in the sea star—a member of the phylum Echinodermata to which chordates are supposed to be related.

1. In the lancelet (amphioxus) pouches are formed in the wall of the gut. These eventually lose their connection with the gut and become hollow tubes running down the back of the embryo. They expand to provide mesoderm, and their hollow interiors constitute the coelom.

2. In the frog solid mesoderm breaks away from the gut and splits internally to form a coelom.

3. In the chick wings of mesoderm flow outward from the axial region. This mesoderm appears to have come from the outer layer and is not derived from the gut. Mesoderm splits internally to form a coelom.

4. In the sea star mesoderm is first extruded into the cavity between the existing germ layers from the gut wall. Subsequently, outpocketing from the gut takes place, forming the coelom.

The above example illustrates that in embryology as in other comparative studies there are similarities, but this does not confirm the doctrine of common ancestry; we explain these similarities on the basis of design. In addition to the similarities there are certain differences in the fundamental patterns for development of the disparate groups. These differences among processes of embryogenesis are less frequently stressed by those engaged in comparative studies; but they are very important, and along with similarities may be interpreted as part of the design.

BIOCHEMISTRY

One of the areas of comparative study which is newer than anatomy[4] and embryology is biochemistry. In this field significant studies attempting to determine relationships among organisms have been produced subsequent to the nineteenth century. Some of the methods used in this field involve the use of blood. Blood proteins can be compared to determine degrees of chemical similarity. These blood proteins are found in the serum of the blood which is derived from the clear fluid in which the blood corpuscles are suspended. It is this portion of blood fluid which does not clot. Hence if a quantity of blood is allowed to coagulate, a straw colored liquid eventually seeps from the clot. This is the serum, and contains most of the blood proteins involved in such experiments.

Let us suppose that we inject some human serum into the body of a rabbit. The rabbit will react to this serum and will build up an immunity to it. This immunity is expressed in certain proteins (primarily gamma globulins) in the blood serum of the rabbit itself. We can then obtain from the immunized rabbit some serum (anti-human serum). When this is mixed with human blood serum a cloudy substance, or precipitate, will form and perhaps even sink to the bottom of the vessel. If anti-human serum is mixed with a serum chemically

---

[4] For a discussion of comparative anatomy, see section on "Similarity and Ancestry" in chapter 2.

similar to human serum, less precipitate will form during a specified period of time. If anti-human serum is mixed with a serum chemically dissimilar to human serum, a slight precipitate may form. If we add rabbit anti-human serum to the blood serum from an ape, a monkey, a cat, or a chicken, we see *less* precipitation than we saw when the immune serum reacted with the human serum. Compared with human serum in an actual experiment, percentages were as follows: ape-69 percent of the precipitation that human serum caused; monkey-22 percent; cat-6 percent; chicken-0 percent (see Figure

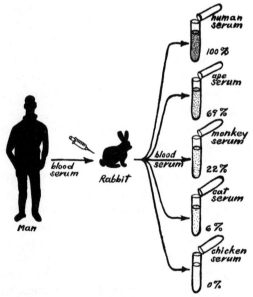

Figure 3—determining chemical similarities in blood serums by precipitation.

3). As one might expect, the more alike organisms are in their anatomy, physiology, development, and the like, the higher the percentages of precipitation are in such tests. In other words, if a number of animals all belong to the same family grouping, they will show more similar percentages among themselves than they will with members of another family. Animals which are similar in other ways can be shown in this way to be similar in their blood chemistry.

At times Christian authors have criticized these types of serological studies on the grounds that some results have indicated relationships radically at variance with reasonable taxonomic ideas. These criticisms, directed principally against *early* twentieth century serology, now are outdated because modern procedures have greatly refined the earlier methodology. Serological technics should be thought of as *methods* (like measuring by rulers) for obtaining comparative data.

Another biochemical method popular in recent years is that of electrophoresis. The apparatus used for this process consists of a positive pole (anode) and a negative pole (cathode) at opposite sides of a mixture of chemical substances which have been obtained from the organism to be tested. Here again blood serum with its mixture of proteins is commonly used. After the mixture is exposed for a given time under a given set of conditions (temperature, pH, etc.), the protein constituents are found to have moved toward the anode, or toward the cathode; or they are found at the starting position, depending upon their sizes, shapes, and electrical charges. At the end of the experiment a certain sequence of protein groups may be observed, and this pattern can be reproduced. Results obtained with a sample from one individual of a species as a rule will be like that obtained from each other individual of the same type. The electrophoretic pattern for one type of plant or animal may be compared with the electrophoretic patterns of other similar forms, and relationships can be inferred when resulting patterns are the same or are very similar. Results have been found to agree with accepted divisions in nature based upon other lines of approach, including anatomy. In addition, various precipitation and electrophoretic studies have proved valuable in situations where differences of opinion have existed, and in certain cases they have suggested the necessity for reevaluation of anatomical data.

As an example of the above, the snapping turtle common in many parts of the United States has long been recognized as anatomically similar to the alligator snapping turtle of the lower Mississippi drainage basin. When biochemical tests are employed using these two forms, results show them to be similar yet distinguishable. Thus the anatomical *and* biochemical data point investigators to concordant conclusions regarding similarities of the common and alligator snapping turtles. Taxonomically both have been placed in the same family but each in a different genus. During past decades taxonomists have considered snappers (including common and alligator) to be closely related to mud turtles. Within the past few years precipitation and electrophoretic research have suggested that the popular classification of snappers into a familial relationship with mud turtles is not as sound as classifying them in closer relation to certain emydid turtles. Some anatomists now favor classifying them as closer to emydids, but some do not. So the biochemical data, along with certain anatomical data, provides a clue to this family relationship problem. The answer to this question, and other similar ones, is reached only after many lines of evidence are accumulated and carefully evaluated.

In recent years tissues and body components other than blood have been used with similar results, and in the botanical realm extracts from seeds and other parts of plants are being utilized. Certain specific proteins like cytochrome C and even the genetic material in the nucleus of each cell, named DNA, have been employed in comparative biochemical research. Basically the purpose of all these studies is to compare for similarities and differences the large molecules found in corresponding structures or fluids in animals and plants. Other similar studies have dealt with the biochemical pathways traveled by these and other chemicals in their synthesis and breakdown. By using information gained from these various approaches it is becoming easier to classify plants and animals into their natural groupings—that is, their basic categories of creation.

Studies using chemicals like serum proteins are basically similar to studies of anatomical structures such as bones, except that in chemical research comparisons are made at the level of large (or macro-) molecules. As a rule the molecules are invisible and so they usually have been studied in group reactions. Also some specific molecules (e.g., insulin and cytocrome C) have been characterized. Classification based upon research dealing with molecules is termed molecular taxonomy. Some have inferred evolutionary relationships because of existing similarities, but as indicated in our foregoing discussions, particularly that on anatomy, these similarities may result from design and can be used to determine the basic groupings found in nature.

BEHAVIOR

A yet more recent field of endeavor which should be included in a treatment of comparative studies involves behavioral patterns; as a science it may be considered a branch of psychology. In these studies considerable stress is placed upon instincts, that is to say, the patterns of behavior which are inborn and are transferred from the parents to the offspring in the same way that various body structures and functions are passed on. A good example is the means by which many birds, reptiles, and mammals scratch their heads with a hind limb. Many animals do this in a similar pattern. The dog, resting on three legs, reaches one hind leg forward to scratch. The bird, while resting on one foot, lowers its two wings assuming a tripod position like the dog, and then scratches its head with the claws of the other foot. Such similarities have been cited in support of an evolutionary hypothesis. Behavioral studies of this sort have been made especially on **certain** groups of birds. Where similar behavioral patterns are found among organisms having like structural equipment, such evidence may rightly be interpreted as indicating the pattern of creation. Similar behavior may be expected in animals that are similar in other ways.

Some similarities of behavior may exist simply because there is only one way to perform a given action. Perhaps birds and dogs scratch behind the ear with the hind leg because the dog can reach the spot most efficiently with his hind leg, and a bird *has* only hind legs. We must recognize, however, that some behavior may not be inborn. The capacity or potentiality might be latent, but the actual behavior might result from trial and error experiences at an early age. The activities are complicated because of interaction between organisms and environments. Nevertheless, certain scientists are making commendable efforts to simplify studies of behavior. When carefully evaluated, data coming from their research may aid in clarification of existing patterns in nature.

4

Occurrence of Organisms and Life

GEOLOGY

THERE ARE REALLY only two philosophically defensible views of the origin and development of life. These are organic evolution and special creation.[1] Supporters of both views must accept the valid evidence, although they may differ on the *interpretation* of that evidence. In the last analysis the most concrete evidence we have is that of the fossil record, and all theories must be considered in relation to it.

Since the creation of our earth various mechanical and chemical processes have made their marks on its crust. In the upper part of the crust are found many evidences that life existed a long time ago. The remnants of this early life are known as fossils, whether they are mammoths frozen in ice, petrified material such as wood, footprints, leafprints, or even tunnels left by worms. Dating of these fossils has never been an easy task. Often various finds have been assigned to ages which are considered valid for other organisms found in the same locality or stratum of rock. Other

---

[1] In theory, various combinations of the two are possible, but the authors know of no view of origins that does not embody *at least one* of these ideas. Nor do we know of any view that embodies a fundamental idea of origins other than these two polar concepts. Historically, organic (and for that matter, inorganic) evolution has been the only alternative to the older view of special creation. Hybrid theories have, for the most part, been proposed subsequent to the publication of *The Origin of Species.*

dating methods, such as radioactive dating, and (formerly) measurement of salt accumulation have also been used. Significant from our standpoint is that at a certain time in the supposed geological calendar, popularly called the Cambrian era, are found a host of fossils which are virtually absent from older layers of rock.[2] From a scientific standpoint alone it is evident that a spectacular event must have occurred at this time. It seems reasonable that the abrupt change at the period designated as Cambrian is a result of God's creative activity.

Also important in our considerations is the well-known fact that gaps are found between major categories of plants and animals in the fossil record. That is to say, various fossil materials may be classified in definite groups and links between these groups are unknown. Over a hundred years ago Darwin recognized the importance of gaps. He realized that these gaps weakened his general theory, for he wrote:

> . . . and this, perhaps, is the most obvious and serious objection which can be urged against the theory. The explanation lies, as I believe, in the extreme imperfection of the geological record.[3]

If, as Darwin thought, the answer did indeed lie in the imperfection of the geological record, one would expect more thorough collecting to reduce or

---

[2] A number of very small fossils have been reported as being Precambrian such as structurally simple alga-like and bacterial microorganisms fossilized in Canadian rocks.

[3] C. Darwin, *The Origin of Species* (6th ed. with Introd. by W. R. Thompson; New York: E. P. Dutton & Co., 1956), pp. 292-93.

eliminate many of the gaps formerly thought to exist. But increased collecting over the decades has failed to eliminate these many gaps. It is true that several organisms such as *Seymouria, Archeopteryx* and *Peripatus* have been cited as intermediate or linking forms, but many enlightened zoologists rightly, we feel, consider them as belonging to separate and distinct categories, only remotely related to other forms if at all. On the whole, the discontinuities have been emphasized with increased collecting. There appears to be little question about the fact that the gaps are real, and it seems increasingly less likely that they will be filled.

Two major theories have been proposed by evolutionists to account for these conspicuous gaps. The first is Goldschmidt's saltation theory (macrogenesis) in which an organism "jumps" from one category to another. The second is Simpson's quantum evolution theory which postulates that rapid shifts occurred between adaptive levels. Commendable as they may be, these efforts to devise adequate models for spanning gaps have, we feel, served primarily to emphasize that natural groupings *do* exist. Every theory, including our own, carries particular problems with it, but many problems contained in other theories disappear when one does not feel impelled to span the gaps.

It is of interest that a variety of forms found as fossils are nearly identical to similar forms living today. A few examples are coelacanth fishes, the *Sphenodon* "lizard," the opossum, metasequoia trees, the mollusk *Neopilina,* the brachiopod *Lingula,* the king or horseshoe crab *Limulus,* and certain ants. Most organisms have shown some variation within the fossil picture. Similar variations become apparent when fossils are compared with types living today. Both in the fossil record and among living organisms certain *basic groupings* are found. These basic groupings of animals or plants possess many characteristics in common and seem to have been constructed according to a basic creative design with modifications in each case that fit the organism's mode of life in changing environments.

BIOGEOGRAPHY

Biogeography, or the distribution of organisms, is another topic which has some bearing upon evolutionary thought. By studying animals or plants which inhabit a specific geographical area it *seems* possible to trace or to ascertain common sets of ancestors.

It is thought that at one time there were considerably fewer representatives of the major groups of animals than exist today. Hence relatively few animals spreading out geographically from the centers of their origin would tend to diversify and to occupy the various habitats available in their new area. Evidence of diversification of a few basic types to fill available ecological niches can sometimes be found.

A classic example of this principle is Darwin's finches. Among the birds on the Galapagos Islands Darwin discovered a group of finches having a range of small to large beaks. The peculiarity of

these birds was that they were obviously related, all
being finches and all sharing similar color patterns
and the like. Darwin suggested that a few birds
which chanced to arrive at this isolated region had
given rise to many descendants which changed as a
result of natural selection into the variety of Galapagos finches of modern times. This is a good example of diversification which is well documented.
The changes seen here are very limited, however,
and they do not justify extrapolation to *macro*evolution, which is concerned with the origin of basic
stocks. We believe that the basic stocks were derived from created organisms.

Marsupial pouched mammals of Australia and
pleistocene South America must have arisen by diversification from a number of common ancestors
which lived originally in the areas where their
modified descendants are now found. But since the
two continents were relatively isolated from the rest
of the world, even more specialized animals were
not able to invade them until later times, when
they decimated the native populations.

In some cases it has not been easy to explain
present distribution of animals from available information on possible routes of migration. Good
examples are the South American and African distribution of certain rodents, or the South American
and Madagascan distribution of certain reptiles.
Animals are found in their present geographical
areas because of migration to (or possibly creation
within) particular restricted provinces. Within
these restricted provinces minor changes could account only for a limited amount of diversification.

Biogeography has brought to light much material which is difficult to explain. The facts cited by evolutionists to support their theory may be open to alternative explanations. There is a pressing need in the field of biogeography for more Christians to do research and to interpret carefully all available data.

THE NATURE OF LIFE
AND ITS SYNTHESIS

Evolutionary studies have involved considerable research and discussion concerning the basic nature of living things and their origins. To date, it has been easier to describe life than it has been to define it. There are a number of features that distinguish living from nonliving material (living —protoplasm—uses food, grows, reproduces, etc.). Actually we can find nonliving models that do all of these same things, for a car uses gasoline (food); a pile of soil *grows* bigger as more is added to it; and a drop of oil, water, or mercury will break into little droplets like the original (reproduction) if it is dropped onto a smooth, hard surface. It is even possible to construct so-called "models" of life, or preparations which closely mimic some of the vital properties of living things. For example, if a drop of strong glue is placed in tannic acid solution a membrane forms around it. The membrane will swell (because of osmosis), and burst; then a new membrane will form around the extruded contents. This behavior has an interesting resemblance to the form of cell reproduction called *budding*.

The answer to the question regarding a main difference between life and nonlife appears to lie in the area of complexity. In nature—in "the dust of the earth"—we find nonliving materials which contain the same common chemical elements (about twenty of them) found in living substance. The difference lies in the way these elements are put together—the complexity of the living material being far greater. Protoplasm consists primarily (about 99 percent) of four basic elements: oxygen, carbon, hydrogen, and nitrogen. These elements are joined to make up organic compounds, namely fats, carbohydrates, proteins, and nucleic acids, all of which are based on the element carbon. Of the organic substances proteins are the most complex and probably play the most important part in life processes.

Building blocks of proteins are chemical units known as amino acids. There are about twenty kinds of these, and they are joined in various combinations to form proteins ranging from about 6,000 to about 10,000,000 times the weight of a hydrogen atom. Many thousands of amino acid units are joined to form most proteins, and the complexity is so great that we know the structure of only a very few small proteins. Living things contain hundreds and thousands of such proteins working together in the life processes.

The formation of proteins appears to depend upon the nucleic acids, namely the deoxyribonucleic acid (DNA) of chromosomes and ribonucleic acid (RNA). The chemical structures involved are very complex in both unicellular and multicellular animals; and the intricacy of the interrelationships among the many substances functioning within even a single cell is only dimly understood. Life is extremely complex, but we are coming gradually to understand more of its marvelous mysteries.

Only life produces life, and there is no scientific evidence that the appearance of life from nonliving substance (spontaneous generation) occurs today or has ever occurred. Results of experiments by such men as Redi, Pasteur, and Tyndall during past centuries, and experiments by a host of living scientists have demonstrated under all sorts of conditions that life comes only from life. Probably this is the best-established law in the field of biology.

However, even though the very simplest living organisms are produced by others like them, many scientists have set up experiments to determine how spontaneous generation could have occurred. On the basis of their results, "models," that is, hypothetical reconstructions of conditions on the primitive earth, such as the thermal model of Fox, have been constructed to indicate how life originally might have come into existence. A typical model starts with an atmosphere lacking oxygen and containing a fluid composed of substances such as ammonia, methane, cyanate, or amino acids. The fluid may be experimentally subjected to heat, electric discharges, radiation, or ultraviolet light, thus causing the simple molecules to join in forming larger molecules and groups of molecules. Such experiments have produced interesting data, but it has not been possible to synthesize anything even closely resem-

bling a self-reproducing organism from simple substances. Many of the basic chemicals used in living
systems such as polypeptides, sugars, nucleotides,
and adenosine triphosphate (ATP) have been syn-
thesized. But if we compare these with a living
creature as we know it now—for instance a single-
celled protozoan, the ameba—the difference is comparable to a few spare parts and an automobile.
However, the results of the experiments directed toward synthesis of life have served to increase our
understanding of life and its chemical nature.

It appears that the hurdles that prevent the development of a self-reproducing bit of life are for-
midable, even in the light of our best procedures
and most sophisticated equipment. Some of our
best scientists are expending great efforts in this
field in order to surmount the barriers which face
them, but so far no life has been produced either
intentionally or unintentionally. If we cannot produce life intentionally, then how unlikely it is that
it could ever be done by accident. However, many
scientists are of the opinion that life came into existence by chance. This cannot be proved, as we cannot prove that life came into existence by the hand
of the Creator. But we accept the latter of the two
explanations, which is in accord with God's revelation in Scripture, as more logical and satisfying.

It has been suggested that the relatively simple
virus which is composed only of nucleic acid and
protein might be a link between the nonliving and
living worlds. But this does not appear valid because a virus does not possess the ability to reproduce itself. Outside of a living cell a virus is subject
to forces which eventually destroy it. Inside a cell

its sole function appears to be the supplying of information necessary for its own duplication at the expense of the living cell. In the words of Dr. Gish, ". . . this in itself must presuppose the existence of an entity capable of utilizing that information, an existence that must have predated the virus."[4] A virus may represent what was at one time a normal constituent of the cell, but because of some change (mutation) escaped from the cell's control mechanism while still depending on the cell for reproduction. It may also, of course, have been created in essentially its present form. In any event, it is unlikely that viruses existed before cells, since they require cells for their reproduction.

Because even the most "simple" forms of life are extremely complex from the scientific standpoint, we do not anticipate the synthesis of life in the foreseeable future. We accept by faith the revealed fact that God created living things. Whether He did this in ways represented by physical and chemical models now popular among molecular biologists, we do not know, and there does not seem to be any way of knowing for certain. Our belief at present is that God simultaneously created those substances (nucleic acids, proteins, etc.) which are so intricately interdependent in all of life's processes. We have faith in the God who created and sustains this universe, and scientific studies have increased our appreciation of this creation.[5]

---

[4] D. T. Gish, "Critique of Biochemical Evolution," *Creation Research Society Quarterly* (1964), I, 11.

[5] Men like Julian Huxley, who said that every biological phenomenon could be explained by mechanistic models, gave evidence of considerable faith—faith that God does *not* exist, and faith in a self-sustaining universe. Such men prefer to reject the evidence of God's existence. (See Romans 1.)

5

The Study of Man

THE STUDY OF MAN (anthropology) may be approached from either of two major directions. *Cultural* anthropology deals with man's patterns of living, especially his social life. *Physical* anthropology deals specifically with man's present physical body and its past history. Anthropological studies most relevant for our consideration are those which deal with similarities and differences existing between man and certain other creatures. Man has developed various patterns of culture largely because he is not bound by instinct, is very flexible, and has great ability to think, learn, use symbols, and talk.

Among the lower animals instinctive behavior seems to predominate over noninstinctive. Even communication and other phases of social behavior possessed by animals cannot be divorced from their involuntary and instinctive reactions. It is true that the basis for man's behavior is to some degree instinctive, but no one would intelligently argue that because of this he is the same as animals. To do so would be to ignore the vast differences between him and the rest of creation and to emphasize small similarities out of reasonable proportion. The differences of degree which *do* separate man and animal are so great that they appear to indicate differences of "kind."

The capacity to learn is found throughout the animal kingdom. It is well known that vertebrates, and even some invertebrates as "lowly" as worms which have been investigated, will readily learn new behavior patterns. Learning can be characteristic of entire populations of animals. Monkeys can learn new food habits by imitation, a rudimentary "cultural" phenomenon. Even the social organization of certain animals has features which cannot be entirely attributed to hereditary "instinct," but are subject to change based on learning. However, man's capacity for learning is incomparably greater than that of any nonhuman creature, including even dolphins and anthropoid apes. Learning experienced by animals may be based more or less upon various vocalizations, but language as an art seems to be restricted to human beings. Although as Aristotle pointed out, the earliest learning in human beings is for the most part imitative, the bulk of the knowledge acquired by adult members of a human society has been due to language.

Many animals are able to communicate feelings based on their present condition and to some extent on their past experience. Creatures as diverse as bees, blackbirds, chimpanzees, and dolphins, have been involved in studies of this sort. Sometimes the communication patterns may be largely learned. An example is the song of certain birds which cannot be sung to perfection unless the young bird has matured in the company of more skilled practitioners. Nevertheless, symbolic language which refers to objects or concepts *not directly evident to the senses* is believed to be exclusively a human trait.

Characteristically human beings produce artifacts or tools typical of their particular culture. Then by means of language or other symbolism, combined with precept and example, they transmit their toolmaking skill to their offspring. For this reason the study of tools has been very important, especially in cultural anthropology. Today most anthropologists believe that man's possession of a culture signified by his use of various tools (such as stone implements in the case of fossil man) is sufficient to distinguish him from all nonhuman forms of life.[1]

Many animals use simple tools. For example, certain wasps tamp down the earth of their burrows with stones held in their jaws, and certain birds and apes use pieces of wood in obtaining food. Some patterns of tool use, or even simple tool preparation, appear to be instinctive but others are learned. Man, however, is the only being capable not only of tool invention, but also of the symbolic description of tool manufacture, making extensive technology possible. Institutionalized means for symbolic transmission of the technology are characteristically found in human societies.

Some have assumed that differences between man

---

[1] It is conceivable that nonhuman toolmakers existed in the past, as in the case of *Australopithecus (q.v., infra)* who does not seem to have been anatomically human, but who may have made tools either instinctively (as a wasp builds its nest of paper) or as an aspect of some kind of "cultural" tradition. Recently, tool manufacture has been observed among chimpanzees in the wild. At this writing, it appears that traditions of tool use and shelter manufacture are indeed learned among these apes, but are learned by imitation rather than by symbolic language.

and animals with regard to learning, thinking, talking, and other aspects of cultural behavior including toolmaking are differences in degree or quantity rather than in kind or quality. Even if this were true, the differences are immense. By most standards a great gulf is fixed between man and beast. For all practical purposes, the culture of man stands entirely alone.

Some have felt that the existence of only quantitative differences between man and beast is insufficient to create an absolute distinction between them. Even if this were so, there *does* appear to be a definite qualitative difference between man and beast in the faculty of religion, or spiritual nature. Man may properly be described as a religious being. He is even more characteristically and constantly religious than he is rational. Religious ideas are found in all known cultures, and thus we feel justified in regarding religious capacity as a fundamental human characteristic. Worship of the supernatural among any creatures other than mankind is unknown. We carry within us that hunger which makes our hearts restless. As St. Augustine has written, "Thou hast made us for Thyself, and our hearts are restless till they find their rest in Thee."

It is our contention, then, that the primary touchstone of humanity is the capacity for religious experience and expression. By this criterion it might be possible for a creature to possess some kind of culture but lack humanity. The remains of a being from an extinct society might differ from modern man in some respects but still be human if capable of religious experience. This circumstance sometimes exists, as we can ascertain from archeological data.

The existence of various discontinuities between man and the animal world has forced evolutionists to explain how this gulf was bridged by evolutionary processes. Most contemporary anthropologists think that mankind evolved from tree-dwelling ancestors who descended to the ground and became terrestrial. Such an ancestor would have resembled a simian much more than a human being of today, but would not, of course, have been exactly the same as a modern great ape. Two basic "choices" were open to this protohominid, as some call him. He could have become a browsing, forest-dwelling animal like the modern gorilla. In that case he would have required a heavy body and great strength to force his way through undergrowth, and like the gorilla he probably never would have fully adopted the two-legged or bipedal stance.[2] With the forefeet needed for locomotion they would not have been free for tool use. Thus the intellectual stimulation which accompanies the origination of a technological culture would not have been open to him. In that case, high intelligence would have had no more value for him than for any other beast (some of which, like rats, do very well without it), and natural selection would not have developed it particularly.

---

[2] Many of the characteristics of mankind are related to bipedalism. Some of these are the curvature of the spine, the shape of the pelvis, the placement of the foramen magnum of the skull, the relative length of legs, and the presence of a well-developed gluteus maximus.

The alternative choice was to become an inhabitant of parkland or veldt, where low vegetation and ground cover is at a minimum. This is the choice that many evolutionary anthropologists believe the protohominid actually took. Studies of baboons and lower monkeys which pursue such a life today tend to show that the use of a simple digging stick would have more than doubled the food supply of those animals. That baboons do not ordinarily eat meat is probably due (at least partly) to their lack of a cultural tradition favoring it. Most monkeys and apes can be trained to eat and to like meat as a dietary item, but it forms no substantial portion of their diet in nature. If baboons had some way of capturing and killing other animals, particularly large game, their food supply would be greatly increased. It is easy to see that baboons which developed a tradition of tool use for food-gathering and hunting would have a great advantage over those that did not, and would so successfully compete with their less endowed colleagues that within a number of generations only tool-using baboons would exist. This would be true even if the tool users were not especially more intelligent than the nonusers.

Nevertheless, once a tradition of effective tool use was developed, natural selection would tend to favor those which could use the tools most efficiently— that is, most intelligently. In this way, culture would favor the development of intelligence, and intelligence would permit the development of a more sophisticated culture. If a faculty of communication such as speech could be developed in conjunction with this, the whole process would be facilitated greatly, and the earth, we presume, would be inherited by the advanced baboons.

We want to emphasize that the foregoing hypothetical story on baboons and other stories like it which have been used to depict prehuman history are speculative and lack hard supportive evidence. There are no bones, arrowheads, or any other finds which impel belief in such a story. The type of evidence we *do* possess is twofold: (1) fossils of various extinct primates and certain forms of man, and (2) remnants of the cultures of some of these in the form of chipped stone implements and the like. From these two types of evidence we may draw conclusions about early man.

The following is a summary of some of the major types of fossils that have been considered to bear close relationship to modern man. This is not intended to support in any way the teaching that man has evolved from subhuman ancestors. Careful reading will show that we intend to demonstrate the humanity of certain fossil forms, and where this is not possible (as in Australopithecines from Africa), to show the absence of a connection with the human race.

1. *Australopithecines* (including *Australopithecus, Zinjanthropus,* and *Homo habilis*). These are regarded as the most primitive of the hominids, or manlike primates. There seem to be many varieties, and a lively controversy is proceeding at this time as to their proper names and the relationships that they bear to one another. For

our purposes it is sufficient to note that many of these remains appear to be too recent geologically to have served as the ancestors of man, even according to the evolutionist's conceptions. Others appear to have had a jaw too narrow to permit the tongue movement necessary for articulate speech. They also lack the "genial tubercles" necessary for the attachment of the tongue muscles by modern man in speech. Some of these Australopithecines in the past were thought to possess a material culture, but at this writing the artifacts associated with their bones are open to alternative explanations and interpretations. One which has been proposed is that the cultural artifacts are the products of Pithecanthropines (see below) which hunted and ate *Australopithecus*. In our opinion, no evidence has yet been presented that is so compelling as to incline us to suppose that *Australopithecus* was a cultural animal, or that he was ancestral to man. Even if he were somewhat "cultural," that alone would not be sufficient to make him human or even near-human (see pp. 66-68).

2. *Pithecanthropines*. These are creatures of approximately human stature and posture which for the most part have been found thus far in the Orient, although traces of their former presence seem to exist in Africa and Europe (Heidelberg man?). It is almost beyond dispute that these creatures had a material culture consisting of hand axes, perhaps spears or digging sticks, and fire. Their cranial capacity was generally smaller than that of modern man, although some specimens approach or meet the lower limit of modern man's brain volume. In our opinion it is possible that these creatures were human, although there is no clear-cut evidence yet that a religious life existed among them.

It is possible that they were a specialized or degenerate branch of humanity.

3. *Neanderthaloids*. Recently it was shown that these people stood as erect as we. Their cranial capacity was as great and often greater than that of modern man, but their forehead was lower. Furthermore, their skeletal structure differed from ours more than those of living races differ from one another. The Neanderthaloids were responsible for the so-called Mousterian chipped stone culture—a culture that was shared by some Cro-Magnoids who were indisputably human. It has been suggested that the Neanderthaloids were a specialized race of people who perhaps were isolated by glacial action and whose physical characteristics were influenced by inbreeding and selection for a cold environment of Northern forests. Thus it would have been desirable for them to be able to climb over fallen tree trunks with greater agility than we would be able to employ. Grave sites of Neanderthaloids have been found which are very similar to those of modern "primitives," and which seem to indicate a religious life of some sort in the Neanderthaloids comparable to that which accompanies burials in some modern nonliterate cultures. It is our opinion that Neanderthal man was entirely human, although racially distinct. It is even possible that people of Northern European descent may count him among their ancestors. It is of interest that the least human-appearing Neanderthaloids were not the earliest of them, but the latest; and that (in early postglacial times) when contact between Neanderthals and *Homo sapiens* became possible, a number of populations (for example, at Mt. Carmel) seem to show evidence of hybridization between the two. The evidence is more than suggestive,

therefore, that Neanderthal man is a portion of the human race that became temporarily isolated by natural events.

4. *Cro-Magnon man.* This was a human being in every respect and was doubtless our ancestor— an ancestor whom we can be proud of. His artistic sense (within the framework of the media available to him) is unexcelled to the present day. There is ample evidence both of high intelligence and a sensitive spiritual nature in him. His religion apparently involved fetishes, sympathetic magic (judging from his cave paintings,) and still other practices recognized by anthropologists as existing among modern culturally primitive societies. In many ways the culture of some Cro-Magnon peoples equals that of the modern Eskimo. Unfortunately, there is ample indication of the darker side of human character among them. Cro-Magnon man seems to have fought and killed those of his own kind and Neanderthals as well.

Evolutionists have been unable to demonstrate that any of these forms have been ancestral (in the evolutionary sense) to modern man, or to other extinct varieties of hominids (with the exception of Cro-Magnon and Neanderthal, who were obviously human). We are therefore unable to see how the fossil evidence here reported can be in conflict with the first chapters of Genesis. Australopithecines were almost certainly not human beings, and the other forms were probably various specialized off-shoots of the main trunk of human ancestry.

We believe that our first ancestors were human in every way and were created in precisely the manner described in the book of Genesis. The variety of human races and types today attest to the relatively small changes which have taken place in humanity since that day. The changes from man's earliest fossil races to modern racial types seem to constitute an example of diversification. From the time of the first man to the present there certainly have been some changes, and apparently these occurred rapidly. But the evidence does not indicate a transitional series beginning with the lower primates and leading to human beings.

6

The Bible and Creation

IT HAS BEEN THE PRACTICE of many religious writers (and even some scientific writers such as Kerkut) to criticize adversely the doctrine of evolution without offering alternatives. Such criticism serves a valuable purpose, but it is the responsibility of the Christian not just to criticize but to criticize *constructively* and to propose alternative views with less shortcomings than those of evolutionary theory. Such a theory, to be adequate, must take full account of all scientific data. And if it is to be Christian it must additionally accept and build upon biblical revelation as valid information.

For the Christian there is no higher authority than the Bible, the inspired Word of God. It is the means by which God has chosen to communicate with man. The method of biblical exegesis (interpretation) most universally accepted among scholars of all shades of theological opinion today is called the grammatico-historical approach. The basic principles of this method are little more than common sense. Among them are the following:

1. Scripture should be interpreted in its own right, and no effort should be made to inject current theories into it.

2. Scripture should be interpreted so as to ascertain as much as possible the meaning intended by the Holy Spirit who inspired men in its composition (II Tim. 3:16).

3. Scripture should be interpreted by taking into account the grammar and vocabulary of the original language in which it was written (primarily Hebrew for the Old Testament and Greek for the New Testament).

4. Scripture should be interpreted in the light of the historical conditions in which it originated.

Sometimes these principles are known as "inductive Bible study," for by them we seek to discover what the Scripture has to say for itself rather than attempting to read our own prejudices and opinions into Scripture.

It is not our purpose here to discuss the various detailed theories formed in attempts to harmonize the biblical creation narrative with scientific discoveries. The first two chapters of the book of Genesis contain the primary biblical information on the subject of creation, and this portion of the Bible has been the object of numerous books and articles by many scholars. At the present time not all Christians are agreed regarding the interpretation of all that is written in these sections, but in spite of this we would emphasize certain outstanding truths in this portion of Scripture.

First, God is the Creator. His power and will are manifested in His bringing of the earth and all living things into existence.

Second, there is order in the creative activities. There is a division of six days, the seventh being the original Sabbath on which no work was done. On the third day plant life was created; on the fifth, birds and sea creatures; and on the sixth, various kinds of animals and finally man himself.

Third, the creation of man was the climax of creative activity. Man was last in order but first in importance. As a living being (soul) he shared the "breath of life" with other created things; but stamped with the image of God, he possessed a spiritual nature that made him unique among all forms of life.[1]

There has been considerable debate among Christians regarding the length of the days referred to in the creation account. Some attempts have been made by evangelical scholars to interpret the days of creation in such a way as to bring them into accord with current concepts of geology. The authors are not entirely unsympathetic with these efforts, but do feel that they often have involved attempts to impose an a priori structure upon the interpretation of Scripture. This procedure is con-

---

[1] Sin entered the human race after the first man disobeyed God, thus bringing about the fall. Sin is not to be thought of as a reversion to any prehuman behavior patterns. It is characteristically human and confined among all organisms to humanity because it involves a violation of moral responsibility which was given only to man.

There are biblical reasons for rejecting an evolutionary account of man's origin. For instance, Eve was formed from the body of Adam, and Adam himself was molded by divine transmutation from some type of earth (see Leupold, *Exposition of Genesis,* pp. 114-16). Descendants of the original man and woman, as well as other creatures, have been subject to change in a limited sense by diversification.

trary to the aforementioned hermeneutical procedure requiring the interpretation of Scripture to
be as inductive as possible. Even if the days in the
creation account *were* lengthy periods of time, evolution still is not taught by Scripture (although
long "days" might *appear* to be more congenial to
the idea of evolution than twenty-four hour days).
We do not desire to delve into an extensive exegeti-
cal discussion of Genesis days, but at present we
feel that the clearest and simplest rendering of appropriate biblical passages is that the days of Genesis were comparable to our own days. We also believe that these days reflect the temporal order of
creation, and we naturally agree with Bible scholars who recognize internal harmony among the various biblical passages dealing with creation.[2]

Genesis chapter 1 contains some very important information regarding the pattern of creation
as we have discussed it previously. The word translated "kind" in Genesis 1 (*min* in the Hebrew) is
used to refer to general reproducing groups of organisms (see Gen. 1:21, 24-25). The term probably
does not refer to "species" in most cases, but it may
refer to genera, families, orders, or other taxonomic

---

[2] Believing in the inerrancy of Scripture, we are not sympathetic with the position of those who believe that the
events recounted in Genesis 2 contradict the account in
chapter 1. Our position results from a profound conviction
that they are very much in harmony with one another. Genesis 1 deals with creation in general, showing man's place
in the large pattern. Chapter 2 treats the creation of man
in more detail. Some scholars would translate certain verbs
in Genesis chapter 2 in the pluperfect tense, as "Out of
the ground the LORD God *had* formed all the beasts of the
field and all the birds of the air" (Gen. 2:19, Berkeley Version). Contradictions disappear when this is done.

categories. The classification that we now use is essentially that devised by Linnaeus some two hundred years ago and is very helpful. But there is no reason to think that the word "kind" as used by Moses about 3500 years ago is synonymous with our word "species." "Species" does not correspond to the word "kind" in our language today. Recent studies by Hebrew scholars indicate that the Hebrew word *min* (translated "kind" in the King James Version) may be much broader in its meaning than our word "species" and may correspond to such groupings as family or order in the Linnean system of taxonomy. It may even have no exact twentieth century equivalent.

It is the task of evangelical research to determine the nature of the Genesis "kind." We may infer that all changes take place only within boundaries set by the creative hand of God since the Scriptures teach that organisms reproduce after their kind. Hence no change can take place capable of causing an organism to move to a kind different from that of its ancestors. For this reason it is important to discover what the boundaries of the "kinds" are.

Summary and Conclusion

THE SO-CALLED "FACT OF EVOLUTION" cannot be proved from the data used by evolutionists to support it. The theory of evolution is, in fact, neither satisfactory nor entirely plausible. Much factual data is inconsistent with the theory in its present form. Arguments for evolution fall into historical and comparative categories. The historical argument treats the geological study of fossils, and the comparative argument treats similarities of anatomy, physiology, biochemistry, embryology, and behavior among organisms. The comparative argument proceeds on the working assumption that similarities tend to indicate common ancestry.

Christian scholarship has scarcely begun to attack this mountain of scholarly study, but there are strong indications that the evolutionary structure is not sound. The raw data used by evolutionists can be interpreted satisfactorily within a creationist framework rather than an evolutionary one. In nature organisms occur in certain natural groupings with minor discontinuities or gaps between these groupings. The Christian need not be burdened with an evolutionary compulsion to explain how gaps could have been bridged. Some similarities may exist between organisms due to their common ancestry, but most similarities are due to their creation by one Designer.

The Christian can present special creation as an alternative to the doctrine of organic evolution. It is his responsibility, however, to explain the *extent* of the changes which may have occurred in animals and plants since the time of their original creation or since the flood. In connection with this responsibility, two major questions must be answered:

1. What is the nature of the "kind" mentioned in the book of Genesis? To what modern taxonomic units, if any, does it correspond?

2. What are the limits of the changes which have occurred among living things as a result of diversification within the kinds?

It is the conviction of the authors that these questions are susceptible to certain laboratory analyses, and, the Lord willing, we intend so to attack them.

The Christian daily experiences the presence of Christ in his life, and he testifies to others of the spiritual power imparted by the Holy Spirit. In everyday living he encounters those who are standing in opposition to the Bible and trying to live with a nontheistic world view. These non-Christians also are endeavoring to dispose of the idea of creation and thereby of their personal responsibility to the Creator. The Christian with a sound position on creation not only will best understand and appreciate nature, but also will have a most effective apologetic and evangelistic ministry to those outside the church. Therefore all Christians who are interested in science should be sufficiently challenged to take part in development of such a position. Perhaps as a result of a renewed research effort by God's people, clarification of His creative pattern will soon be forthcoming.

For Further Reading

Note: This list is intended as a guide to further investigation of the questions we have raised. Naturally we do not endorse every book on the list as being completely sound doctrinally or scientifically. Those which we feel we can especially recommend as being theologically wholesome and scientifically accurate are starred.

American Scientific Affiliation. *Modern Science and Christian Faith* (2nd ed.). Wheaton, Ill.: Van Kampen Press, 1950.
This book was prepared by conservative scholars and deals with the relationship of the Bible to many fields of modern science, including creation (316 pages).

Balyo, J. G. *Creation and Evolution.* Chicago: Regular Baptist Press, 1961.
A popular introduction to the problem posed by evolution, this book is written by a Christian pastor for the evangelical Christian (23 pages).

*Clark, R. E. D. *Darwin: Before and After.* Chicago: Moody Press, 1966.
By a Christian scholar who, with strong historic emphasis, points out many adverse intellectual, social and other consequences of Darwinism (192 pages).

Clark, R. T., and J. D. Bales. *Why Scientists Accept Evolution.* Grand Rapids: Baker Book House, 1966.
Using many quotations from selected leaders in evolutionary thought, the authors emphasize that philosophical (including antisupernatural) convictions have played a significant role in the acceptance of evolutionary doctrine (113 pages).

DeBeer, G. *Embryos and Ancestors* (3rd ed.). London: Oxford University Press, 1958.

This author is a scientist and an ardent evolutionist, but in this book criticizes the embryological recapitulation argument. The discerning reader can find much here which has anti-evolutionary implications (197 pages).

*Keil, C. F., and F. Delitzsch. *The Pentateuch,* Vol. I, *Biblical Commentary on the Old Testament* (reprint). Grand Rapids: Wm. B. Eerdmans Publishing Co., 1949.

This volume contains an exemplary commentary on Genesis written by Keil, the more conservative of the two authors (501 pages).

Kerkut, G. A. *Implications of Evolution.* New York: Pergamon Press, Inc., 1960.

Although written by an evolutionist, this book has strong anti-evolutionary implications. The approach is primarily scientific and treats mostly invertebrate and biochemical data. The uncertainty of the general theory of evolution is demonstrated. A must for all biologists (174 pages).

*Klotz, J. W. *Genes, Genesis and Evolution.* St. Louis: Concordia Publishing House, 1955.

Written by a conservative Lutheran scholar formally trained both as a scientist and as a theologian, this book deals comprehensively with almost all scientific disciplines relevant to creation and evolution (575 pages).

————. *Modern Science in the Christian Life.* St. Louis: Concordia Publishing House, 1961.

This book covers many scientific topics of importance to the Christian, including a section on creation and evolution (191 pages).

Lammerts, W., *et al. The Challenge of Creation.* Caldwell, Idaho: Bible-Science Association, 1965.

A symposium containing papers by six authors, this work is a popular approach to the biblical view of creation and evolution. The point of view is factual, with emphasis upon creation interpretations (80 pages).

*Leupold, H. C. *Exposition of Genesis*. Columbus, Ohio: Wartburg Press, 1942.

A monument of conservative biblical scholarship, this book is thorough, logical and exemplary. We believe it is the best commentary available on the subject (1220 pages).

*Marsh, F. L. *Evolution, Creation and Science* (2nd ed.). Washington, D.C.: Review and Herald, 1947.

The author is scholarly and scientific in his presentation of a sound creationist viewpoint. This and the following work are only two of the several worthwhile contributions by this Christian biologist. He is especially noteworthy for his treatment of the problem of Genesis "kinds" (381 pages).

————. *Evolution or Special Creation*. Washington, D.C.: Review and Herald, 1963 (64 pages).

Mixter, R. L. (ed.). *Evolution and Christian Thought Today*. Grand Rapids: Wm. B. Eerdmans Publishing Co., 1959.

Papers by a group of Christian men of science, some of whom seem to accept modified evolutionary doctrine (224 pages).

Morris, H. M. *The Twilight of Evolution*. Grand Rapids: Baker Book House, 1964.

The author is a conservative Christian civil engineer who is strongly anti-evolutionary and favors flood geology. He uses much Scripture, this constituting a strong point in favor of his work (103 pages).

Murray, D. *Species Revalued*. London: Black friars, 1955.

A work by a Roman Catholic entomologist who points out weaknesses in evolutionary ideas together with the manifold invidious effects of Darwinism (166 pages).

Nilsson, H. *Synthetische Artbildung. Grundlinien einer exakten Biologie* (2 vols.). Lund, Sweden: Gleerup, 1953.
Written in German with an extensive English summary, this book is the work of a Swedish botanist who opposes macro-evolution primarily on scientific grounds (1303 pages).

Reno, C. A. *Evolution, Fact or Theory?* Chicago: Moody Press, 1953.
This book is a conservative Christian discussion by a biologist. It is intended for high school students. A revision is in preparation (127 pages).

Thompson, W. R. *New Challenging Introduction to The Origin of Species.* "Santhia," Stoke, Hayling Island, Hants, England: Evolution Protest Movement, 1964.
With some added notes this booklet contains Thompson's introduction to the Dutton & Co. (Dent & Sons, Ltd.) 1956 printing of Darwin's 6th edition of *The Origin of Species.* Reasons are given for doubting evolutionary doctrine and for feeling that Darwinism has not been beneficial (20 pages).

*Zimmerman, P. A. (ed.). *Darwin, Evolution and Creation.* St. Louis: Concordia Publishing House, 1959.
Papers by four conservative contributors who are scientists, theologians, or both, covering the subjects of creation and evolution. This book is perhaps the best comprehensive discussion of the problem and is both biblically conservative and scientifically sound. We heartily recommend it (231 pages).

Excellent papers are often found in the publications of the Creation Research Society, the American Scientific Affiliation, and the Victoria Institute (England). The addresses of these organizations are listed below. Since these are periodicals and contain the contributions of many authors, we are not in a position to completely recommend them all, but, we caution our readers to evaluate them carefully and critically as they would other writings. The interested reader may also derive much benefit from the Doorway Papers of Dr. A. Custance, Box 1283, Station B, Ottawa, Canada.

Creation Research Society
2717 Cranbrook Road
Ann Arbor, Michigan 48104

American Scientific Affiliation
324½ South Second Street
Mankato, Minnesota 56001

Victoria Institute
12 Burcote Road
London, S.W., 18, England

The Case for Creation
Subject Index